A Way Home

OREGON ESSAYS

Scott F. Parker

Drawings by Alex Hirsch

Portland, Oregon
David Oates, General Editor

Published by Kelson Books
2033 SE Lincoln
Portland OR 97214
kelsonbooks@gmail.com

Book and cover design: Steve Connell/Transgraphic

Printed in the USA

ISBN 978-0-9827838-3-2

Library of Congress Control Number: 2018942123

For my families.

The reality I had known no longer existed.
—Marcel Proust

CONTENTS

GOING HOME

In the life cycle of the salmon there comes a time when the fish has reached maturity that it will return to its place of birth to begin the next generation's cycle. In Oregon, each salmon will swim upstream, sometimes hundreds of miles, from the deep Pacific, locating one stream out of thousands in the region. It's one of nature's seeming miracles. We don't know what combination of temperature, magnetic, stellar, and chemical cues is involved, but a carefully calibrated olfactory system is a necessary component. Sadly for salmon of recent generations, the acid, heavy metals, and pesticides we have put in their environments act to disrupt their sense of smell, making it less and less likely that a salmon will find its way home.

It makes me wonder what factors might be disrupting my own navigation, because every time I return to Oregon it isn't the home I'm looking for. Like the salmon, I'm trying to locate the place I was born. And as with the salmon, I fear that place is inaccessible. I don't know where this instinct in me to keep returning comes from, but it is strong, and year after year I make return trips aimed at the place I left, each time discovering that a steady accretion of incremental changes has resulted in a complete discontinuity.

Unmoored this way, I think of a story I read as a boy about a man in whose house it was a different time in every room. This troubled the man greatly until he acquired a pocket watch that he carried from room to room checking the time in each room against it, not against the other rooms' clocks.

What can I carry with me when I return to Oregon that will orient me in a smilar fashion? Something that even if it doesn't lead me to my origin will at least allow me not to be so lost. It seems there's a tradition of essential longing that long precedes me. Writers who look out to find a world that does not match up with their ideas of it. I think of Basho:

> Even in Kyoto—
> hearing the cuckoo's cry—
> I long for Kyoto.

Perhaps he is one of my ancestral salmon, and my instinct for home an instinct to compose a lost one. Home, I imagine that place:

> Even in Portland—
> gray clouds obscuring mountain—
> I long for Portland.

FUTURES

They say Minneapolis is the first city of the West, but *they* always seem to be coming from the East. For Sandy and me, setting out from Portland, Minneapolis was the last place we could call West.

We planned to spend two years in Minnesota, but the two have turned into four (and probably more) the way they can. Strangers have become friends, friends have become some of the dearest people to us in the world; and Oregon, season by season, has taken on an increasingly and unmistakably Edenic quality: an idea of a place we'll never return to. And these Minneapolis years have become, by a considerable margin, the longest we've lived in one place.

But today I'm on the Empire Builder, the Amtrak train that runs west from St. Paul to Portland—or, as we're taught to think, across all the open space of America between history and destiny. And even as the sun sets ahead of us like a falling target, last night I had to cross east over the Mississippi River to board the train—my metaphors telling me I must go back before I can go forward (the going forward already a going back). Sandy dropped me off at midnight. She's staying in Minnesota for the summer to work and take care of the cat while I roam about Oregon.

I like to think that if this were a story I would know my role in it. But as it is not a story, merely what is happening—in a word, *life*—I cannot account in full for what brought me here or where I'm headed, to say nothing of what any of it means. Maybe one day it will all make sense, sense ever lagging experience, sometimes indefinitely.

Sandy comes from a family of movers. Joining that long tradition of western optimism, she spent her childhood crisscrossing Wyoming at the call of her father's work, *home* ever to be for her a fluid concept. Since she left town after high school, never to return, her parents have gone on moving: to an unincorporated town in northern California, to suburban Oregon, and to Texas hill country.

Mine, however, is a family of stayers. My mother has been a Portlander for half a century, and my father has spent his days almost exclusively between Laurelhurst and Irvington in Northeast Portland; among his six siblings, none settled farther away than Olympia, Washington, from their childhood home on Laddington Court, and two landed within three blocks of the house they grew up in. The house my parents live in, a full two miles from Laddington, is the same one they bought when my mother was pregnant with me and there was still ash from Mount St. Helens in the gutter.

I find nothing unusual about my family's situation. If the West is a restless place, west of the West, the Northwest can feel a settled one. We are strangely dreamless about moving on, almost un-American in our contentedness to stay. Growing up, I never got the news that New York was the center of the universe. And a tropical paradise— Hawaii, say, or Mexico—was fine, but only for a week or so before it would get to be "too much." We held no fantasies of California—a quick look around the neighborhood revealed that everyone there was hurrying to get here. Only in college, when I started to spend time with people who weren't from Oregon, did I first hear complaints about the rain. My understanding of *home* is colored by the fact that it never occurred to me to want to be somewhere else. There's no greener grass than what grows in the Willamette Valley. At the risk of sentimentality or of mythologizing the West: I feel fortunate for my roots.

Yet I left Portland. The reasons weren't mythic or even romantic: no ricocheting off the Pacific with the momentum of Manifest Destiny behind me. Where I grew up, such progress was synonymous with history—it had served its purpose. When I left, it was for the ordinary reasons: opportunities and commitments: grad school for Sandy, an itinerant writing life for me.

My inheritance does include elements of the past. It is my mother and my father's father who are directly responsible for bringing what would become the two halves of my ancestry to Portland. Mom came out from Bozeman, where she'd graduated from Montana State University, to attend the University of Oregon Medical School (now Oregon Health and Science University). It was with something akin to the pioneer spirit that she was one of the first women to matriculate at her school, her interest in medicine inspired in part by her mother's long-term suffering from multiple sclerosis. She was on the frontlines of second-wave feminism and faced regular dismissal from some of her male colleagues accordingly ("You're taking a real doctor's spot here"; "I can't believe we are wasting an education on someone who's just going to go have babies"; etc.).

Grandpa Steve (Stephen E Parker at the time, Ellsworth Sterling Parker by birth, self-reinvention being only one of his archetypally American traits) came west with his young wife, Helen Louise Scott (known later to me as Grandma Cookie), seeking opportunities unavailable on the family farm.

Before his death five decades later Steve recorded a series of interviews that his oldest son drew from in composing *Hard Work and Seren-*

dipity, a short biography distributed among our family. The book presents an ambitious young protagonist who basically hustles his way from Depression-era poverty into numerous jobs and journeys as far afield as what is now Pakistan. He saw Gandhi speak in India, steered clear of Mussolini in Italy, was briefly arrested in Istanbul under suspicion of being a Soviet spy, and ended up in law school at George Washington University despite not ever having finished college. A few years later, after graduating from the University of South Dakota, where he transferred to be closer to home, this young witness to history found himself in Sioux City, Iowa, with a law degree and a wife, ready to finally make his future happen. "You see," he says, "our home in South Dakota had been very humble. We didn't have many fancy effects. I'd traveled so extensively that I knew people have things, and I wanted them. I wasn't content to live the way my ancestors had lived."

He took a job with the insurance company Aetna, hoping for an assignment in Minneapolis. Instead, he was assigned to Portland, a far-off town he and my grandmother allowed would provide adventure. Her journal from the trip west confirms their hunch: "Friday [4/28/39] found us on the road at 7:30 again, with Ogden as our immediate objective. Our progress was impeded on several occasions when we encountered huge droves of sheep being driven by sheep dogs and by men on horseback to the spring ranges. Literally, our car was engulfed at times with sheep milling all about us."

My grandparents drove west before the Interstate Highway System was established. Riding the train in 2013 from where they had once hoped to make their lives to the one where I knew they were grateful they had, I feel an affinity with their journey. I look out from the Empire Builder and can nearly see from their perspective the gradual unfolding of this slow westward crawl.

The Columbia River they drove alongside, before The Dalles Dam went in in 1957, featured Celilo Falls—treacherous to pioneers floating the river this stretch of the Oregon Trail, sacred to native peoples for millennia. Out the windows of their passing car there were "Indians whom we could see out on the rocks spearing and trapping in nets the large salmon" that "annually make the pilgrimage from the ocean up the river to spawn." Another fifty miles along the way, at the Bonneville Dam, which had gone in just two years before: "We were amazed to see that some of these salmon were three and four feet in length, but natives have told us that they oftentimes grow to be five or six feet long and weigh as much as sixty pounds."

This history is accessible to me now only through written reports and warped photographs, but I feel sometimes like it only just eludes my memory. These are places I know, people I knew; yet it is all so wholly foreign to my experience: Indians spearing giant salmon and catching them out of the air as they leap up the falls—ancient traditions still being practiced in full view of curious white onlookers headed for the city.

But some things are for me as they were for my grandparents: "The Columbia River Highway from The Dalles into Portland," Louise writes of the final leg of their journey, "takes one through the heart of the most rugged and majestic scenery in America, according to many world travelers, including William Lyons Phelps of Yale. In this contention we are willing to concur." She would

have been in good spirits to concur with such a sweeping claim so eagerly and with so little basis of comparison. If she played the optimist in foresight, Steve, later in life, was happy to play it in hindsight. Recalling their first drive into town, he said, "I felt right at home the minute I got here, felt like I'd lived here all my life. Everything was *déjà vu*."

However much I trust such statements as reportage, I admire the courage of their optimism. It's an optimism that feels foreign to my generation, despite how we have been encouraged to understand the future. This advertisement excerpted from my fourth-grade Oregon project, *Pioneer Life in America*, reveals how even very recently we have been taught to see our state: "FREE LAND"; "YOU CAN START OVER"; "GREAT CROPS"; "IT'S WORTH THE TRIP."

Because this West is at least as conceptual as it is geographical, those of us born here must ask where we can go from where our ancestors were trying to get. Where are *we* trying to get?

If this were a story it'd be the one where the disparate parts of my life add up to one coherent self driven by one identifiable purpose. We went to Minnesota looking for a future. And now four years later we are still looking. My grandparents had been looking for a future too. And they'd found one. But they are decades gone now, their futures with them.

It could not have been otherwise. When you're young there is only one future and you're always headed right for it. But futures belong, finally, to the dead; for the living they are as elusive as the horizon: histories waiting to be told by those who will find themselves beyond their reach.

I'm learning to take all stories with a grain of salt, especially when I'm standing in the company of their heroes. The mythology of the American West, notable as the most recent telling of the mythology of America itself, is of opportunity and entitlement to it. To go west is to seize fate. From what or from whom fate is being seized usually goes unsaid. Our ideals require the kind of blank slate we don't find in the messy contingencies of real lives. Real lives of exploitation, of scarcity, of destruction. Not to mention the psychic burden that comes after you get what you wanted and discover it isn't enough. And never will be.

Our myths, dating back to the Enlightenment and all the way to the uncoupling of mind and body, are myths of control. They have allowed us to become very rich in the short term. In the long run, as the material success of the West helped us forget, this will destroy us. Our faith in progress will be its own undoing—if not for all, for most. You don't get far down the tracks without thinking the future isn't what it used to be.

Too much we live as if we're independent of our environment, yet nothing exists without that which it exists in. Still, we go on without giving care to the future because our worldview presupposes the ability to start over at all times. We are meant to start from zero. This is fantasy. Everyone starts somewhere. But pretending otherwise allows us to keep moving toward the proverbial West, the West of our desire.

William Kittredge has been one of the voices declaring our need for a new mythology here. "We need to invent a new story for ourselves, in which we live in a society that understands killing the natural world as a way of killing each other."

Kittredge is good company this twilight with rain drops beading on the other side of the window inches from my head as the Empire Builder climbs through the Rockies. The best thing about traveling—especially traveling by train—is the precious time for uninterrupted reading. This trip to Portland is two days, and I have a bag full of books. They feel like friends. And some of these friends are closer still, residing in my consciousness: Robin Cody, in whose *Ricochet River* I found needed consolation for my own boyhood losses; David James Duncan, whose *River Why* revealed the mystical wonders of a young man in tune with his environment; Ken Kesey, his *Sometimes a Great Notion* so big as to make space for everyone who would come after; Kathleen Dean Moore, her gentle footsteps in *Riverwalking* leaving a path my mind still follows; all of them contributing to my Oregon.

There is soft lightening on the horizon. The green lakes of Glacier disappear around me. I close my eyes, lean up against the glass, and settle in for the night, my thoughts mixing with dreams as sleep comes over me.

When Sandy and I were a year out of college and between low-paying jobs, we took a road trip, unhurriedly following our whims from Portland to Minneapolis. This was four years before we would move there. Along the way we passed through Bozeman and Yellowstone and learned that if you follow Highway 212 far enough east off the park's Grand Loop Road you'll end up on the stretch known as the Beartooth Highway, at nearly 11,000 feet the highest elevation highway in the northern Rockies. According to the highway's website, "the Beartooth Highway crosses some of the most extreme country in the world." You leave the historical and enter the geological as you rise up from pine forests to glacial lakes the color of liquid air and then to the barren alpine tundra hospitable to almost nothing, certainly not you.

Weather is eternally in play in the Beartooths. "Severe weather" occurs even in the summer, when a day of seventy and sunny can bottom out into snowstorms and freezing temperatures in hours. The road is normally plowed by Memorial Day—though closures are common through June—and remains mostly open until early fall. Winter comes early up here and it comes quick, like the off flick of a light switch. Unless you're the kind of person who travels with contingency plans, extra water, and space blankets, you've got no business.

And if you're like me this is the kind of information you dig up after the fact. In the moment of action, the only plan Sandy and I had was to drive around looking for moose, which we'd heard were commonly seen drinking from the alpine lakes. It was a good plan, one of the best we'd had since leaving Portland.

But gas was running low and we were a ways still from Red Lodge, the next town. The glacial lakes were behind us. Up there only tundra, stray boulders scattered over treeless mountaintops, a desolate and forgotten place. We were caught in that space of not knowing whether we'd crossed into real danger. The sky had darkened ominously by the time we reached the blockade where the road was closed. September's as good a time as any for winter to start. If this were a story, now would be a good time to note that the temperature had fallen twenty degrees from an afternoon high in the mid-fifties and seemed likely to continue falling, and that the snow was now coming down in fat and moist flakes that obscured visibility enough that for a moment we could pretend we were somewhere else.

But this isn't a story, it's only what happened, and we didn't know yet how serious it was. Often you don't know until it's too late to do something about it. The mountains, the snow, the moose if they were around, the cold, indifferent universe, Sandy. How serious was this? There was no contrast: what was dangerous, what was not. I couldn't imagine how we'd get out. We needed something or someone to come in from offstage. God or a kind stranger. We might have found either out there. Why not? Or we might have had the great good fortune of a downhill leading back toward gas and a car just efficient enough to get us there in time.

If this were a story the resolution here would offer a bit more than the observation that for the time being we are still alive.

I promise myself I will tell this as a story eventually, preferably as comedy: Sandy and I have a brush with danger, escape, come out on the other side, where we are free to revel in the happily ever after of the very future we had hoped we were aimed at. For all I know this will even be a true story.

The Empire Builder is somewhere near Pasco when I wake up and see the water. We are following the Columbia as it bisects Washington. As the train rollicks through the gorge I look out across the blue river to Oregon and watch as the brown hills give way to the green and greener forests north of Mount Hood—those deep and enduring woods—and before long the lush verdant Willamette Valley I stubbornly call home.

ON THE GENTLE SAND FACING IN

or How You Never Stop Becoming Who You Are

0.

Ocean rain. The winter day is somber, as the rain pulses hard and soft with the wind against my face. The gray majesty of the Pacific stretches before me and I feel the wetness seep under my jacket and into my socks. It's all so familiar. What's not familiar, as I walk the trail up from the beach to the town of Gearhart, is the inland view.

1.

The time seems right, we tell anyone who asks why we're getting married now, vaguely alluding to nothing in particular. If pressed, we'll move closer to the truth, adding something about wanting to formalize our relationship publicly for the friends and family we care so much about. Part of the way we see marriage is as a decision to live primarily not for each of us but for *us*. And in the move from *I* to *we* is a move to the larger *we* of community. There's a duty we inherit to the traditions and conditions that bore us—not a duty in the sense of an unwanted obligation, but duty as an opportunity to align who we are with the values we aspire to. And if that's an abstract way to frame love and our deepest earthly commitments, it's also a sincere way.

The decision to marry made, practical questions remained: When? Where? Who to invite? Our best considerations eventually converged on a small ceremony on the beach, followed by several days visiting with friends and family who would join us in Gearhart. I called a rental agency and reserved the house at 138 N Ocean—the house that for over thirty years had been my family's.

2.

Longtime resident Millard Rosenblatt writes, "Gearhart is like 75 years passed it by. I think Gearhart is the most remarkable place because it is so unchanged. . . . The little changes that have occurred are relatively small compared to the rest of the world."

I remember when it was impossible to imagine that Rosenblatt could ever be wrong in this assessment. I remember being young and looking forward to a future that would resemble my then present. The Portland I was born into, I could tell from an early age, would not be the Portland I'd grow up in or later return to. But Gearhart, I thought, would always be Gearhart. When a winter storm spectacularly reshaped the dunes, it was still the beach; when John Allen opened his cafe, there was still no McDonald's in town; when the Wiederhorns seized their own land from public use, it was, after all, their land; when Grandma Cookie died seven years after Grandpa Steve, their house stayed in the family.

3.

My grandparents purchased their plot of land in Gearhart in the early sixties, then saved money so that when they eventually built a house there they could pay for it in cash. The house, completed in 1969 and painted a soft wooden gray that blended with the neighbors' homes and the sleepy quietude of the town, sat on the corner of First Street and Ocean Avenue, which street names rightly indicate the choiceness of the location. Kitty-corner southeast was a square block of open grass where as kids my cousins and I played soccer and Frisbee and sometimes baseball. East of the park were two public tennis courts, where we learned how to hit flat old tennis balls with our parents' warped wooden rackets. To the park's west, immediately south of the house, was an undeveloped tangle of shrubs and blackberry bushes, where we built forts connected by elaborate passageways that lasted the seasons. This land opened up to the tract of beach grass, a quarter-mile wide, dividing the city's growth boundary from one of Oregon's treasures: publicly owned beaches, accessible to all, running from Washington to California.

For years, we cousins ran wild over that land, racing through the beach grass that poked our bare legs and arms as we made our way atop the highest bump between home and sea, a bump we christened Strawberry Hill, and from which we could see clearly south a few miles down the beach to Tillamook Head, the small mountain that runs directly into the ocean between Seaside and Cannon Beach, and we could see off into the northern distance as far as the day's cloud cover allowed, sometimes (in breaks from gray) miles and miles of blue against tan or, turning slightly to the left, a wall of blue where sky and sea never abutted but merged to reveal for us one world reaching from some infinite horizon all the way back over us to the atmosphere we could breathe and feel cool against our faces and see actually *from within*. We were the sea those days.

There was little time to enjoy the view, however, or reflect on our fortunes, as the urge to play overwhelmed us. This was true back at the house as well, where the part of the basement that wasn't devoted to economic sleeping spaces was left for recreation: pool, ping-pong, darts, and board games. In the closet were two pairs of boxing gloves the three of us boys would take turns wearing to slug one another in the face until someone got a bloody nose or the invisible line between boxing and fighting was crossed and screaming, flailing rage broke loose. It might be half an hour after such a scene until we were

43

sworn allies again, and in the meantime we'd join the neutral adult world upstairs. Nothing, no matter how painful, took very long at the beach to be made idyllic. Worries had a way of fading into the distance in Gearhart.

4.

Sandy and I met in college. It took me two years to get her to go out with me, but once she did it was only a few months before we decided to move to Colorado together after graduation. I was never so eager to choose the future, sure as I was that it would include, not replace, the past.

That same spring, my dad called me in Eugene to say that he and his siblings had decided it was time to sell the beach house. This disappointing news came to me as no surprise. We'd kept the house under joint ownership since my grandma died nine years before, but it was becoming increasingly hard financially to maintain it.

The house was in decent shape, but needed repairs and could stand some modernizing. No significant work or refurnishing had taken place on it since construction. Not needing to be in Colorado until August, I went to Gearhart in June to spend a month painting, gardening, ripping out carpet, and coordinating with contractors on some of the bigger repairs we wanted to make before putting the house on the market. Sandy, still living in Eugene at the time, drove out to meet me when she could. I showed her the changes to the house; we held each other close and looked out at the ocean, excited by what was before us. But there was a sadness in me too, a fear that it would never get any better than this.

5.

I can still feel the quiet emptiness of the house at summer dusk when the sunbeams angled through the western windows and little clouds of dust hung in the air—it's always September at these moments, always the end of something I want back. In my memory I stare out and watch the sun go down like it's gone down every time I've stood here before. I feel my grandma's presence in these moments. The house has always felt like it belonged to her, like she was the only one in the family who could fill it up. She's sitting in the green swivel chair by the window cracking a Diet Coke, watching me watch it all slip away again. She tells me that I'm young and that I should enjoy it because it's worth enjoying. I do enjoy it, I tell her, but it won't last. When are we ever not watching the sun set? "You think too much."

I can't help it. The sun is resting in my eyes, then my heart, then my stomach—and part of me is still standing there full of sun in a time that doesn't exist.

6.

You can think about life as an experiment. You run the trials, get the results, and recalibrate as necessary. The thing about life, though, is that not all experiments can be repeated. I wanted to marry Sandy at the family house as way to unite past and future in the nexus of her and me. The union, of course, would prove that every harmony is itself the death of solo and every song the death of silence. The experiment was to make it all come together in our own union—and the experiment failed. When I reserved our old house, it was spring, all was in color, cleared for a spotless future. When the property man called a few months later to say the new owner was tearing down the house to replace it with a larger one and our reservation wouldn't be recognized, we were confronted by what we always knew: in our marriage we'd be responsible for not relying on the past but creating the conditions of our future.

Practically speaking, Aunt Martha found us another house down the street from ours, big and beachfront. Sandy and I arrived in Gearhart the day before our wedding and walked up Ocean Avenue to where the family house had been. There, we stared down into a pit of sliding sand, new foundation only cursorily laid. I felt as empty as the hole, knowing exactly what had been taken away. But there was no reason to linger there. Our wedding was tomorrow and everything was up for grabs.

7.

The past has weight. But do I give the beach house more meaning than it had? How could I not? Back when our house stood, it was a place, a place we enjoyed, but still a place, one among many, a fact as plain as any other—in its passing it becomes so much more: it is now history, a *necessary* condition of the world as it is. Without it there would have been no me, no *this* me. There is living, yes, but there is also a having lived.

8.

I shudder at the inland view. The McMansion that has replaced my family's home, simultaneously generic and ostentatious, sits large above the town portending expansion and collapse at once. The small footnote of my family seems erased from

Gearhart's history, but what I see from the beach, ocean at my back, is not that we no longer exist as we did but that history itself will be erased by forces larger still. The environment hums indifferently along, the windswept dunes reshaped by rising tides, the river winding like the trace of a snake across the summer sand, the weathered tennis courts demolished and rebuilt and demolished, time tearing away and replacing only itself.

FREE AND EASY WANDERING ON
THE PACIFIC CREST TRAIL

In the past, and not without reason, Sandy has substituted *foolhardiness* for what I take to be my courage. Nevertheless, after making known her concerns for my safety, she has ultimately endorsed my trip out West to search for adventure while she stays home in Minnesota to work. I've provided every justification for her concern, and here I am headed once again into the woods, haphazardly prepared as ever. I have with me a sense of purpose and a sense of direction, as well as the sense that these may not suffice. The thought briefly passes through my mind that I'd like to be better prepared, but it's really more that I'd like to be the kind of person who could bother to be better prepared. Except even that isn't quite right. There's a reason I create these hardships for myself: I'm drawn to the opportunities they afford. And yet part of me must believe in becoming someone else, even the kind of person who prepares for things. We don't journey alone into the woods *only* for the scenery or peace—or adventure. We journey into the woods so that the scenery and peace and adventure might change us. It's a psychological project, if not also a spiritual one. The rock-bottom appeal of a journey is it literalizes our metaphors. Here we are. And there we go. And how we will get there. And if. The life and the story can be overlaid, harmonized. At least my temptation is to think so.

My plan is to hike 113 miles south on the Pacific Crest Trail from Mount Hood to McKenzie Pass, where I'll hang a left on Highway 242 and do about fifteen more miles into the quaint mountain town of Sisters, where my dad will pick me up Tuesday morning. Right now it's Thursday morning, mid-June, early in the season. I've got a backpack and only the least bit of backpacking experience.

Years ago, I hiked from the Columbia River at Cascade Locks forty miles or so up and around the western side of Hood to Timberline Lodge with my cousin Anna. That section, directly north of where I'm starting now, is the most difficult stretch of the Pacific Crest Trail in Oregon, gaining 6,000 feet over those miles. That's under good circumstances. Under our circumstances it was also raining and miles of trail had been washed away in Zigzag Canyon, where there'd been a major landslide the previous winter. Luckily, I'd hiked—which is to say I'd gotten Sandy and myself horrifically lost in—that section of the trail a few weeks before and knew my way across when I was there with Anna.

That was my first backpacking trip, and I had

subjected my cousin to conversations like:

Me: "How will we carry enough water for three days?"

Anna: "You're hilarious.

Me: "I'm serious."

Anna: "Oh! We'll find streams to drink from."

Me: "Wait. Are *you* serious?"

While mostly I'm amused by my ignorance it carries a bit of shame with it too. Intellectually, I reject the mythology of the self-reliant—often American, often male—individual, but part of me nevertheless remains identified with it and needing to grapple with it. By going alone into the woods and finding my own water, which Anna showed me is fairly manageable in the Pacific Northwest, I will achieve my Western bona fides. This will to prove myself through conquering (nature, weakness) is so embedded in me that I fear any rejection of it is not in fact a transcendence but an admission of an inability to achieve it, the maturation really a resentment. I reject the terms of absolute independence only because I cannot succeed by them. And so, for the sake of my integrity, I must succeed first and turn my back only later. After all, we carry our pasts with us as well as our packs when we enter the woods.

DAY 1

First thing I do in the parking lot at Barlow off Highway 35 on the southeast side of Hood is go off to piss on a tree, this being one of the true masculine joys of outdoor recreation. Then I strap my unwieldy pack onto my back and start walking. On the far end of the parking lot I encounter my first obstacle. There is an unmarked four-way

intersection of trails, two of which directions must be the Pacific Crest, only one of which is the one I'm looking for. I pause, deliberate, pick the one I suspect as most southerly, and hope for the best. Pacific Crest hikers should always carry a compass, I learn the predictable way.

My guess is good, though, and soon I am getting farther away from the mountain and noticing trail signs that confirm my direction. A heat wave is expected to move in tomorrow, but today it's still cool and the air is moist, dense Northwest forest all around me. I settle into a comfortable rhythm, my heavy backpack keeping my pace restrained and steady. Forced to go slowly, my thoughts turn introspective. Do we not always enter the woods in search of a way to be?

The feeling of solitude sets in suddenly. If I don't get too lost, I have 109+/- trail miles to McKenzie Pass and all the hours till then to be reminded how I like living with myself. Some people find this sort of thing insufferable. In his short book *America and Americans,* John Steinbeck writes, "We are afraid to be awake, afraid to be alone, afraid to be a moment without the noise and confusion we call entertainment." Half a century later, the spirit of that statement holds, but the constancy with which we now achieve distraction belies the suggestion that there is some other "real" world to be distracted from. But of course some of us still find it a relief to be alone in the woods. I have nothing but my thoughts to distract me from the task of being awake in my surroundings. Visions of clarity and transformation appear before me and I pursue them into the woods one step at a time.

The trail is well marked and very clear, and if a hike is a metaphor for a life it's one that only plays in retrospect. The metaphor breaks down in the present, as the trail advances in single-minded or single-track direction while the life—my life—is always at risk of going off course. There are even occasional miles signs nailed to the trees—and thank god there's no life analogy here. For years my goal in life has been to be prepared for death when it comes, whenever it comes. I think of Chuang Tzu, who asked how he knew in hating death he was not "like a man who, having left home in his youth, has forgotten the way back?" I often understand myself as a man who is lost, but I aspire to the equanimity to handle what I encounter along my way and to be ready when the trail ends. This is a challenge worthy of a human being, I believe. The ground is rolling beneath my boots these miles, but no major climbs or drops so far. I hear trucks on what must be Highway 26 cutting south from Hood to Prineville. I press on, aiming to get in as many miles as I can while conditions are great.

There's a whole spread of daylight before me and I'm only four miles from where I thought I might end up today, Little Crater Lake. Making good pace. Leisure departs me when I'm alone and my vision tunnels around the trail. I see miles ahead of me and no reason to stop. To smell the proverbial flowers, which in this case are pink rhododendrons. The joy I find in hiking arises from the motion, the rhythm my legs start that spreads to my breathing and my thinking. The surroundings are secondary to the fact of my body moving through space. Analogy to essay: I like the thinking more than the thoughts, and I'm willing to risk occasionally getting lost. Perhaps I would stop if it weren't for the barbaric mosquitoes swarming about. There are other creatures as well—one deer, one frog, a few humans back near the crossing of 26—but it's the mosquitos I really notice as it finally occurs to me where the verb "to bug" comes from.

The trees are starting to thin out as I move gradually into desert, and when an east wind blows it carries juniper and hot dry air. I find a fine-looking stump and sit down to eat my second donut from Joe's Donuts, where I stopped on my way to the trailhead, and demonstrate anger toward the insects. The damn things are not impressed. A troop of Scouts comes along on its way north from Olallie Lake, a five-day trip for them to Barlow Pass. I tell the Scout leader my plan to make Olallie in two days before passing Mount Jefferson on the third. I can't tell if I've impressed him or embarrassed myself, but he wishes me luck in the snow and takes his responsible boys ten miles a day northward.

I make Little Crater Lake by mid-afternoon. It's an idyllic scene, this gentle walk over from the PCT on a wooden walkway over a marsh of purple flowers and fat bumblebees. There is still hope. The lake is thirty-four degrees (I read on a placard) and clear as sunshine. You can see the rocks going deep under to the wellspring that feeds it. I just emptied my third water bottle and I'm in need of a refill. The West has been called the place where the issue is water. Hiking the Cascades, I'm describing the dividing line between that West and the Pacific Northwest, where the main problem with water is that we're all soaking wet half the year. And with no Cousin Anna this time to collect my drinking water, nothing makes me more nervous on this trip than the possibility of dehydration or drinking bad water. I trust my sense of direction and deductive reasoning to get me out of any lostness my carelessness might get me into, and I'll take my chances with a bear (there aren't any grizzlies around here), but I have less than full confidence in my ability to identify safe water. Do I remember reading that lake water is good for drinking because it receives so much UV light? And don't I also remember reading that moving water is preferable? Well, lake water is the water that's available, so lake water it is. I fill all three of my bottles and wait for the iodine pills to do hopefully enough.

I like to think of myself as an outdoorsman. It's an appealing self-image, though the correspondence with reality in this matter is approximate. I do like being out here. And no small part of what I like is the possibility that things can go wrong at any time. Besides, what I lack in experience I make up for in stubbornness. If I have a skill it's for following through doggedly.

And with that, onward.

I stop for a short break as I change out of my hiking boots into my water sandals for my first creek crossing (a feeder into Clackamas Lake, I think). My feet are pale, wet, and wrinkly. Sort of remind me of naked mole-rats. My left foot features a lone blister, my right has a few more (two blood-filled) and my fourth toe is bloody around the nail. I walk into the cool water and feel life returning to my toes.

I'm at about mile 2082, which puts me at twenty miles or so from Barlow Pass. Camp is already set thirty yards off the trail in a sort-of flat opening on the forest floor. I don't know the names of as many trees as a writer should. Nature to me is an ambiguous concept I love to lose myself in. I trust that the trees have names and that there are educated people out there who know them. But naming is not knowing, and description is only sometimes explanation. A name is only what a tree is for us; what interests me about trees is how they are and what they do. I know this about them: they are balm on my wounds.

The mosquitos are back, and I'm too tired to bother much with dinner, so I eat a peanut butter sandwich and tie my pack up in a tree away from any bears that might come looking for a Snickers bar. I climb in the tent and kill the only mosquito that gets in with me. I'm too tired to be a good Buddhist this evening, but I think Chaung Tzu would approve. And it's him whom after tremendous deliberation I've brought as my sole companion. At one point during packing I had as many as five books stacked up ready to go, sure each would be needed at some point on the trek. Symbolic and heavy-handed choices, all of them: Dante, Augustine, Whitman, Thoreau—all left behind in favor of Burton Watson's translated *Chuang Tzu: Basic Writings,* which has the hiking advantage of being lighter weight than the others. Not to mention it's the book more than any other I've tried to live my life by; notwithstanding the paradox of taking direction from an author who communicates in parables, an ethicist without prescription, someone whose best known passage asks whether he has dreamed himself a butterfly or whether he is a butterfly dreaming himself a man. The trick for me would be to not know anything and yet to function— no, *flourish.* And besides, I can't help but bring plenty of other writers bouncing along in my head with me. I open the book up to Watson's introduction and fall promptly to sleep.

DAY 2

I wake up early with a heavy body. My legs are stiff and my shoulders prefer that my arms not be raised overhead. I wonder if I have the strength to haul myself and all this gear across the Warm Springs Indian Reservation today. Of course, I do.

I make four things of oatmeal and one cup of coffee for breakfast by adding the last of the cold lake water I collected yesterday. To save weight, I didn't bring a stove, so everything I'm eating I'm eating cold. Also, I don't own a stove. The cold oatmeal is a fine success, but the coffee holds onto the iodine flavor of the water. Shit. But at least I have come across my first indisputable lesson of this journey: refraining from the wild does have good coffee to recommend it. I dump half of it for the chipmunks and, only moderately caffeinated, load up. The fourth toe on my right foot is big and purple and in no way interested in going back in the boot. But in it goes.

An hour later, as I cross into the reservation, the trees are getting smaller and the sky is getting larger. With more sunlight reaching the soil the undergrowth is more bountiful here. A large gray-brown toad so big it can barely hop stumbles out of my way. A few steps further along a light green tree frog no bigger than my thumbnail hops so big it practically flies off the trail. This is the time of day for wildlife. I keep my eyes to the ground and notice two small piles of scat full of white fur. Can I convince myself it was left by a cougar? I try, but I cannot. No cat would be so indelicate as to shit on the trail and not bury it. Coyotes, though, it would be just their style.

Mid-morning I stop on the trail to eat a PopTart, which one blog recommended. The flavor I have is Double Fudge Chocolate Sprinkle Blast! or some such processed nonsense. Note to self: find new blogs to read.

I find a spring and begin the routine of filling up water bottles and waiting for the iodine to kick in. It's been clear to me most of my life that I'm one of those people who is out here waiting for something to happen, and that something could best be described as hearing god talk through the trees. But if spiritual signals are coming my way I'm not picking them up. My attention extends not much further than the next water source.

To be responsible for your own survival is to be attentive to the elemental foundations of life. I think of water, sometimes I get as far as shelter and food, but if this is its own spiritual lesson (and maybe it is) it's not a transcendent one but an embodied one. Literally: I am body. Which can be an invigorating fact to be reminded of. Days spent searching out potable drinking water, evenings spent hiding food from bears, this does heighten the sense of being alive in a way that everyday screen-saturated life just cannot.

But even so, we are only ever so much "in nature." I help myself to salmonberries as I happen upon them, but the food that sustains me comes with me from the world of commerce and excess. Am I in the mood for Organic Yakisoba Noodles or Garden Vegetable Couscous tonight? Whichever I choose I will simply add water (*Is my water safe yet? How long does the iodine take?*) and in so doing feel the pride of self-sufficiency.

For humans there is only the human world, just as for bears there is only the bear world. Or maybe better to say, for humans and for bears there is only this world: what we make and what we find (whoever, whatever made it). *Natural*— the closer you look at it, the less it means. If the human tendency toward destruction weren't natural then neither would be the creatures who pursue it. Conversely, were we a wiser species than we seem to be, that situation would have been just as natural.

I like for such thoughts to visit me neutrally. If *natural* is a meaningless concept, then whatever is the case is merely what is the case, and the normative claims that the deepest core of what feels like *me* desperately wants to make are but my peculiar commitments, however capriciously acquired. I will declaim the virtues of the wild to anyone who will listen, but when did I take on the assumption that life is entitled to virtues? It's true that we don't miss the bison when we don't think about them. And if we don't tell our children what they're missing, how will they ever know? You can build a society this way. If the world is as it is, I ask myself, what good is there to be upset? Sometimes I answer *nothing*, and sometimes I oscillate back to *everything*.

The water must be safe to drink by now. After a successful night and another successful water collection I'm feeling very confident, like I can do whatever needs to be done. I can drink from lakes and springs, I can dig a hole to bury my own shit. I can climb mountains, cross creeks, talk to the trees. I am appreciating Gary Snyder's "gratitude to it all; taking responsibility for your own acts; keeping contact with the sources of the energy that flow into your own life (namely dirt, water, flesh)." The PCT is the most pristine trail I've been on. Eighteen inches wide, running the length of our American West, and so far not a single piece of trash on the ground. The Bic ballpoint pen I found writes as well as it ever could have and some poor hiker somewhere is disappointed not to record his own best thoughts. It is a valued thing. I gather that those who are inclined to hike here have a deep reverence for the land. And it's this reverence for the land I'd like to extoll more even than the land itself. It's not in its own that the land is valuable but as part of us. And yet in calling attention to this pristine stretch of land, I reinforce the very dichotomy I want to dissolve: in celebrating, I otherize. Nature is good; we are sinners. But the Bic pen is a valued thing and valued things and valued places are two products of the same outlook, an outlook that leads to valued life.

We'll see whether this optimism maintains if I get tired in the afternoon. But for now I am very content here just making my way steadily through the peaceful day.

Five hours and twelve miles in, I stop for lunch alongside a meadow of rhododendrons buzzing with pollinators. In addition to an energy boost, a lunch break will give me a chance to rest my legs and will marginally lighten my load. I can't get used to the metallic taste of iodine water, so it's a delight to have time to indulge by mixing a packet of EmergenC in with my water. For food I open a packet of ramen into my bowl and add cold iodine water. While this softens I eat another PopTart, which has not improved in taste. I'm out of patience trying to keep insects out of my bowl, so I rush to eat the ramen before it's ready. The smaller pieces are softish and only the bigger chunks are fully crunchy. But it goes down just fine. It would probably be best to rest awhile and maybe read some Chuang Tzu—his Master Yu would have something to teach me now about the best uses for my failing body—but there are literally ants in my pants and it's time to get moving.

Been walking three hard hours. It's hot. I don't think I'm sufficiently hydrated. The trail goes nowhere but up. When the mind isn't put to good use it threatens to become a hindrance. As one can't help but notice as life's daily distractions are replaced by what constantly underlies them. Only twenty-four hours alone in these woods and already I'm seeing myself more clearly, noticing the fluctuations in my moods and my attention. According to the environmental historian Roderick Nash, "The solitude and total freedom of the wilderness creates a perfect setting for either melancholy or exultation," and I'm hitting either on the regular. A lookout point that doesn't reveal an overly clear-cut landscape (I've learned not overly clear-cut is the best I should hope for), a good spring to drink from, the possibility, however remote, of encountering a cougar—these are enough to send me into paroxysms of glee. And just as suddenly . . . Maggie Nelson says loneliness is solitude with a problem. My solitude can become an acute loneliness for brief afternoon stretches when the forest goes quiet and still and a wave of fear sets over me that this universe really is inanimate.

My tiny human steps getting me nowhere, the doubt creeps in: Why am I on this hike? Why am I on this life? What do I want to happen on my way through the Cascades? Don't mosquitos ever rest?

A light breeze crosses against my cheek. This will suffice to keep me, pointless or not, walking a little while longer until this web of experience comes fully back to life.

At Jude Lake, where I'll call it a day. I find a small campsite off the trail, discard my pack, remove my shoes, and sit on the lakeshore where I plop and dangle my feet in the cool mountain water. Rest. For fifteen minutes I do little more than wiggle my toes, which is plenty. Whatever else is happening in the world, there's nowhere I'd rather be than soaking these feet in this lake. If there is something better somewhere out there, I'm too content to bother imagining it.

After thinking myself satisfied, I set up my tent and come straight back to sit in the water some more. This time I strip all the way down and dive clumsily in through the lake muck. Wild ducks splash land out in the open water and it's just me and them out here.

It was a tough afternoon. South Pinhead Butte doesn't look like much on the map, but I timed it just right so I hit it at the heat of this hot day. Direct sunlight, dry desert air: maybe I can learn how to be easier on myself.

I climb out of the water, put on my boxer shorts, and resume my position sitting on the shore. My left foot looks the same as yesterday, my right foot actually better except for the fourth toe, which is bleeding on top with a large blister wrapping around the whole bottom and front—hopefully this cold water is helping. Looking down at my submerged feet, I notice a crawdad crawling back to the cover of a log I dislodged. He is bright pink and disappears quickly. I move the log again but cannot find him. Now that I'm looking, though, there's a brown newt a little shorter than a pencil swimming around my toes—maybe feeding off my bloody toe, what do I know? Hungry or not, it's as curious about me as I am about it. I swirl my foot slowly; the newt takes caution and then returns as my toes settle. I saw a garter snake this afternoon. If I hadn't been so tired I might have seen it before scaring it away, as it was lying out on the trail. If it were here now it might go after this newt, the garter snake being one of the only animals resistant to the newt's toxins. One of those textbook evolutionary arms races.

And an hour is gone, but gone where? I am still here. And I am still me. The skin that has flaked away in the water, the blood and pus that have leaked out. The fluctuating reality of "I." I am no more these intermittent fears, lonelinesses, and hopes than I am the pieces of body I leave behind. They vanish in and with the movement of time and what's left is only what's left. In this moment is the totality of "I." Nothing is lacking. And wherever the hour has gone it has taken with it everything that is not happening now. Existence is experience. And experience when you attend to it is enough. Some dark clouds have been moving in, maybe a little rain tonight.

I go up to the tent, eat half my Indian Curry, hang up my pack out of the reach of bears, and lie down. I make it through the introduction this time and into Chuang Tzu's "Free and Easy Wandering" before my mind settles down into my tired bones.

NIGHT

I wake up to the sound of something rustling outside the tent. It sounds small, probably raccoons or mice, but I'm picking up a strong whiff of urine, which is characteristic of bears. My food is up good and high, except that I put the leftover Indian Curry down the trail by a rock so I can pick it up in the morning. Do bears like spicy food, I wonder as I try to sleep, glad that I didn't make salmon.

DAY 3

I peed only once yesterday and that can't be good. My shoulders are stiff like they've been holding up my world, which in a way they have been. But my legs, by god these legs can do anything. I count my blessings and make myself pee. What comes out isn't what it should be but a trickle of fluorescent yellow, and that can't be good either. Three and a half miles ahead I'll leave the reservation and arrive at Olallie Lake, where I'm expecting to find a campground with a general store. Let them have Gatorade.

In the store at Olallie Lake familiar comforts are almost beyond my ken. I buy two Gatorades, a Pepsi, a gallon of water, and get to guzzling. I buy extra oatmeal and some "all-natural" insect repellent, refusing I guess to really believe the word means nothing. I drop $20+ and it's worth it. I drink the Pepsi, one of the Gatorades, and half the water. The rest of the water I use to fill up my bottles.

It's disorienting to see humans for the first time since I left Timothy Lake the day before yesterday. I ask the kid working the store how long it'll take me to pass Mount Jefferson today. He stares at me for an inordinate period of time before telling me that despite working and living here he's never gotten around to hiking up that way. These humans, sometimes I just don't know. Before I go, he hazards a guess, "Maybe a week?" Now I'm the one staring strangely, pretty sure I'll make twenty miles and be coming down the other side before dinner.

Better hydrated, I begin working the base of Jefferson.

Coming up from Olallie is all happy John Denver tunes in my head. Open meadows and strings of alpine lakes, Jefferson right over there. La-da-da life is grand and if I can later see me now I will smile.

Approaching Breitenbush Lake I enter a burned-up valley. It's eerie as shit, a deathly end-of-the-world scene. Some grass patches speak of a future, but otherwise it's charred black sticks speaking only of what happened. Damn. I'm glad to see this. These woods are so tender, this land so precious. I put my feet down gently, humbled.

I'm into the Mount Jefferson Wilderness. No fires allowed here. Not that I have the tools to start one. As I gain elevation the snowpack increases linearly, but the mosquitos do so exponentially. I spray myself down with the natural stuff but it makes no difference. As soon as I slow down I'm swarmed. I eat a Snickers and mix a bowl of cold ramen while I walk, my one arm flailing helplessly about my head. These fuckers are under my skin almost literally—they're biting me through my shirt. I smash them vengefully and to no real purpose. No amount of their blood will satisfy me. And in this we are of a kind. Full of anger, I am sweating sloppily, climbing higher, and thinking to myself it doesn't even matter how beautiful it is.

The snow's getting thicker. I trudge on. I come to a snowfield, look across to where I reason the trail should be and try to keep my aim true. The snow is hard packed and I do not fall through much, but it's slippery wet in this heat and sometimes I slide a little. I plant my walking stick, lean in, and take conservative steps. I'm too close to Jefferson now to see it. Hood is visible to the north. I read in the paper before I started out that there's a climber lost there, and that's a shitty thing to think about right now. But as long as I reconnect with the trail every ten minutes or so I trust I'm moving in the right direction.

I haven't seen any dirt in a while and there's none of the signage I saw in the Mount Hood Wilderness here, so I can't be sure I'm near the trail. I turn my phone on, and though there's no service the GPS function tells me that I'm 300 feet at 242 degrees from the trail. I line up what I can tell about north and south from the ridgeline, guess what three hundred feet means out here, and give it a shot. The GPS now says 117 feet at 60 degrees, so I guess I'm getting closer. I play the guess and check game for thirty minutes and I'm once again feeling pretty good about myself. The voice in my head that expects to make it is still the loudest one, but the voice of doubt—or reason, whatever you want to call it—is starting to speak up.

I've got another thousand feet of climbing ahead of me. I'm still on the northern side of the mountain, meaning I can't count on much more melt until I crest or break the timberline. And when that will happen I don't know. And what if my phone battery dies while I'm still in the snow, as I assume it will? Then I'll be forced to guess without checking. What risks am I prepared to take today?

I lean against a tree and wait for a sign. I'm not aware that that's what I'm doing. But it is. I think I would make it. But if I get off the trail, if I can't tell where I am on my maps, if my GPS dies. Big problems start with small mistakes. I say that I'm troubled by archetypes of conquering and metaphysics of opposition, yet here I am ready to go higher in the mountain with no honest plan for how to get to the other side. And why?

Because I'm seduced by the challenge and the possibility of being my own hero, asserting an indomitable will. But look closer at this will, and isn't it the source of my frustration in the moment? My ideas about what I should do at odds with the circumstances surrounding me. My attachment to a rigid version of my *self*. Without such steadfast preconceptions, where would the problems arise? Not under the high mountain sun. Not in the shade of pines. Perhaps if success means anything on this journey it won't mean conquest but rather the dissolution of the terms of conquest. If I can focus less on a trail I must complete at all costs and more on the experience of being on the trail I can wander more freely and easily. I can even convince myself that in this humility lies a rejoinder to the spirit of dominance that has ruled this land since the Enlightenment swept west. I can convince myself of this, can't I?

I look down at the phone. A single bar of service flashes. Well, I guess there's an escape plan. I open the phone function but the service is lost. I climb a bump and move away from the trees and wave my phone around like a crazy person. When the bar of service returns I call my dad, who says, "Hello? Hello? Are you there?" Nothing I say goes through. I text my sister: "Too much snow. Can't pass Jeff. Tell dad Breitenbush Campground tomorrow. Any time."

I try in vain to get another text out, but the bar of service has vanished. I lean once more against a tree and try to accept the finality of my decision. There is some relief at having made what I think is the right choice, but there remains a feeling of defeat within me. I'm suspended somewhere between common sense and cowardice, and I cannot tell which is closer.

I'm cooling out in the Breitenbush River, but the mosquitos are inside my mind again, which is already buzzing. Did the message go through? Will it make sense? And other such questions I can't answer.

I get out of the water and hike up to the campground. Even though it's hot, I'd rather get in my tent than deal with these mosquitos.

Once the tent is set up, I decide, no, I'd rather deal with the mosquitos than bake in the tent. I walk around the grounds. My legs are so used to motion they don't want to stop. The fundamental component of reality—of human reality at least—is momentum. When it's working for you, there's not much work left over you have to do. But right now my legs and plans are at cross vectors.

I walk over to the mosquito hatch that doubles as a scenic lake and suddenly it occurs to me that something isn't right. Breitenbush is one of the more well-known campgrounds in Oregon, but there are only two other groups here. The rest of the grounds are empty. I approach one of the groups and ask if anyone knows exactly what is the deal. A middle-aged woman produces a map and shows me that we are at Breitenbush Lake Campground, a somewhat isolated campground back in Warm Springs. Eyeing her brand-new Subaru Outback, I ask how far it is to Breitenbush Campground. Eyeing the knife tied to my belt, she tells me it's a thirteen mile hike and if I leave pronto I can make it before dark.

Tent re-disassembled, pack repacked, I head back out. The long road to civilization is a bumpy mess, rocks and potholes, dust and deep ruts. Dad would never try to make it up here in his Camry (if it occurred to him, if he got the message and checked the other place first), so good thing I'm walking it.

Gives me something better to do than wait.

I'm walking my versatile legs along, appreciating that it's all downhill and thinking about why evolution never produced the wheel. No more than a mile in, though, my reasoning is forced to confront the versatility of a four-wheel drive, double-rear-wheel beast. A truckful of guys pulls up and the driver shouts out, "Hey, man, want a ride?"

I say exactly what I always say. "No thanks, man, I got this."

Thirteen, now twelve, miles is nothing I can't do, so why would I want any help? Is my thinking. His thinking turns out to be that it's hot as hell and I'm walking on a shitty rock road. This is only one way in which Tom is smarter than I am. I hop in. Tom and his three buddies are old-fashioned Oregon outdoorsmen in a shiny black truck that I fall for completely. It's roomy

and air-conditioned and built for mountains. The power we have here is exhilarating. Tom and his buddies have hiked and hunted all over the state and know well where I ran into my trouble. Another week maybe, two definitely, they assure me, and I would have made the pass. Too bad, too, it's the best stretch in all of Oregon, they say. We mash over the road like nothing, slowing only to make room for a struggling minivan and pretty soon we're at the campground.

It's not yet dark as I claim the last available site.

Here I am now at my own picnic table, time to sit by the river and really dip further into the *Chuang Tzu* ("There is a beginning. There is a not yet beginning to be a beginning."), time to drink coffee made from non-iodine-saturated water, time to write in this journal. Time finally to sit still. Now that I'm not in a hurry to get further along maybe I can get somewhere.

It is a good feeling to relax and know that as long as communications went through all I have to do is read, write thoughts as they occur to me, and listen to the river. No more studying maps and planning water stops. In the wilderness you must stay aware of wilderness. Here it is enough that there are trees and a river and lovely places to be. Lovely ways to be. *Here*, I note, in a crowded campground, not out in the remote woods. Here, where I can be outdoors at real leisure. The interplay of nature and culture impossible to think about isolating. It lacks a purity—and I should hope so.

I find myself here, the closest thing yet to the self I want to be. Like something I was destined for. What an exhausting thought to think, *destiny*. Every being has a role. The butcher to cut meat, the rooster to crow, the big to be big, the small to be small, the great to be great, this tick on my elbow to be crushed under my pen, the sacred tortoise to drag its tail in the mud. "The whole world could praise Sung Jung-tzu and it wouldn't make him exert himself; the whole world could condemn him and it wouldn't make him mope." I am a man (small) in a land (big). How small? How big? I do not know. I discover my perspective from the ground and sing my songs into the breeze. I'll go down cheerfully, wherever I go. The dead man laughs at the living. Po Chu-i lost his reason for being; he was never happier. I have been here since creation and yet I am a mere fart in the wind. How foolish is this bumbling existence. And what makes a thing so? Making it so makes it so. I speak of things made only because I haven't the words for those unmade. Understand they are no different. Ha! forget your commentaries.

I breathe Oregon air because my mom moved for school and my dad's dad got a job out west. Also in China long ago a butterfly dreamed of flapping its wings. The rhythm of that flapping dictates the meaning—*I vibrate, I vibrate*—the tick finds me large, the trees find me small. What am I? Further vibrations inside vibrations meaning I could go on forever.

I had a hard time turning around. I thought the journey was a failure. I realized, though, I didn't know where the journey was leading, much less if it was a failure. These judgments bring suffering. Edward Abbey, another intermittent Taoist, writes, "It doesn't much matter whether you get where you're going or not. You'll get there anyway. Every good hike brings you eventually back home. Right where you started." Amen and good night.

FIELD NOTES FROM THE
DIFFUSE HEART OF OREGON

KELLEY POINT PARK

How easy for a Portlander to abstract "port." The city comes up here through miles of industry until suddenly the land squeezes between converging waters and you're facing Sauvie Island, left foot in the Willamette, right in the Columbia, the two rivers uniting between your legs. You feel so remote; you are so remote. Lewis, Clark, and co. missed the mouth of the Willamette both coming and going, the island obscuring. The wash of water on the river beach here sounds of the coast to which they were headed. The summer trees cotton the ground. No one arrives by accident these days, so far from "reality" these foundations. The currents here are at cross-purposes—the forces apparent even on the surface. Underneath, hidden, there is so much more; you can trust this, sitting on a bench looking at a display of a cougar standing right here watching explorers and their native guide in a canoe right down there as they venture out.

SOUTH JETTY

The mouth of the Columbia, the Columbia Bar, the Graveyard of the Pacific, 2,000 ships sunk, these three jetties constructed in the late nineteenth and early twentieth centuries to allow safer passage, the South extending farthest into the sea. The journey out to Oregon's northwesternmost point an arduous hours-long climb over miles of seagull-stained boulders, waves crashing in from the Pacific, crabs scurrying at the sight of you, seals living fat, playing in the water below. At the terminus, salt on your skin, water on three sides, terra firma a mirage in the distance behind.

FORT CLATSOP

Over two hundred years ago Lewis, Clark, and co. made their winter camp here, and some of these trees were already ancient. Hiking south from HQ along the Lewis and Clark River (formerly the Clatsop's Netul River), a few miles inland, the sun breaks through—on the coast it's probably raining still. I'm on a large platform/walkway stretching over a marsh with dinosaur-sized leaves growing all around. A little way back, a tree frog; here, Sitka spruce towering, ferns like giant fans, a salmonberry or two to chew on, Oregon grape in bunches, and me seeing and thinking best on the move.

CAPE MEARES STATE PARK

South in the Sitka vegetation zone it's raining again or maybe still depending on what you count as a break, but I'm staying mostly dry under this forest canopy. The moisture is doing wonders for amphibious life, frogs and salamanders in happy abundance. I use a rope to climb the steep pitch down onto the rocky beach where the waves roll up to my feet and the log I'm sitting on, claiming all of what I was already considering *my* real estate. Adventure, of course, means not knowing what will happen next. I begin the climb up from the rising tide, sheer cliffs above me.

CASCADE HEAD

A small patch of blue sky to the south. Thick fog over the head. It's early as I start out under morning mist. Too much rain along the way to stop and take notes, I'm back at the base now, wet as a whale. I startled, and was startled by, one raccoon in the woods on its way home to sleep the day away. Emerging soon after from the first forest section and topping the crest of the head, I looked back to find a small herd of elk coming into the opening behind me where my trail had just crossed. They walked and chewed grass unhurriedly in the morning fog, fog so thick in parts I couldn't see beyond the "dangerous cliff" sign showing a hiker in mid-fall to see the actual hazard, my own fall foretold. Later, on the way down, the clouds slowly opening to reveal cliff, a peregrine falcon on the top of the highest tree

below me, the ocean a soft background hum. The falcon called out loud and distinct several times, then lifted off in a few powerful flaps and soared gracefully up, gliding in tremendous arcs through this unexpected life.

OREGON DUNES

Climbing sand onto sand for hours, the Pacific possibly an illusion retreating as the ground crumbles and slides beneath my feet. The angry roar of off-road vehicles reminds me that the world I imagine is not always the one I find myself in. Nevertheless: these birds, these skies, these directionless days.

GOLD BEACH

The scenic south and warmer water quiet sound.
The Rogue, one of the original rivers nationally
designated Wild and Scenic, moving through
forest and canyon from the Cascades joins the
ocean. But for banana-belt sharks, one might
envision floating luxuriously down coast toward
the California border where the redwoods stand,
incomprehensibly, above the rest.

CELILO FALLS

A small jetty into the Columbia that may mark where the falls sounded across the region before the dam drowned it out, may mark where the native people caught salmon moving upstream for ten thousand years, a sacred place. A newly dead suckerfish lies on the shore attracting flies and bees. Beams braced against crossed supports reach out from the jetty. No signs here. No one really around. Traffic on the interstate moves briskly by. Land is dry brown—bare terrain not a riverbend from the lush valley. Oregon, I'm reminded again and again, is a multitude. Water quite clear and not very cold. If there were fish near the shore I could see them from twenty feet. A particularly turquoise dragonfly, an inch long and thin as nothing lands near a rogue patch of wild blackberries that taste better than what even the co-op can get. What once was a gathering place is now a freeway rest stop, but the wind here is significant and pleasant and I don't suspect it will stop.

JUBILEE LAKE

Driving an hour on gravel roads up into the Umatilla National Forest seeing no one but a few camouflaged hunters, who steward the land better than my liberal guilt ever has, I expect a solitary lake hike. Instead, I find a crowded family campground—cars, boats, fishing, noisy kids, etc.—and a paved trail for half the way around the lake. Still, majestic. Lots of deer. As I sit now to write I hear the sound of something large off to my right. Probably a deer . . . and then from the left a jogger, and the animal to my right goes silent. Jogger unaware of it and me. Things here, they disappear.

WALLOWA RIVER

Up early to head generally onward. Got down into the forties last night and brought on a feeling of fall's onset. I've been driving through mountains and canyons and along this river I'm now sitting by, listening to the light constant rush of one moment leading to the next as the sun rises warm on the left side of my body. I remember everything.

JOSEPH CANYON

Lucky to find a good trail down at the end of an unmarked side road. Joseph Canyon takes its name from Chief Joseph, who likely was born somewhere down here. I'm descending to Swamp Creek alert to the possibility of animals, as this area is known to hold healthy populations of bear and cougar. Plus whitetail, of course. Two bounded by my car on the way here. Nothing doing, though, predator-wise. I see evidence of cows everywhere, but no cougars. If they are out there watching me I'd make for easy prey, exhausted, fumbling up Starvation Ridge.

WALLOWA LAKE

Drove through Enterprise and Joseph, Black Angus grazing serenely over the rolling grass foothills of the Wallowas, to arrive at this transparent lake beneath the mountains. Chief Joseph's father is buried just down the road, right over there. Before dying, he told his son, "This country holds your father's body. Never sell the bones of your father and your mother." Either my eyes deceive me or there's still snow in the crevices above. Could be. The water is cold. It's so cold. I've been in colder, but that's not the point.

Drove several miles into the forest off Highway 3 into what I gather are hunting grounds just south of the Joseph Canyon lookout point, and now I've hiked in a ways farther using my phone's GPS to mark points to lead me back to the car, which I left camouflaged under the layer of dust I picked up on the road in. The big trees have all been taken out of the land and the hills are covered with branches that look to this cautious explorer like potential rattlers. It's funny in a place like this how the mind swings between hope and fear, anticipation and disappointment. I want to see a cougar (or just a snake) but I'm scared as hell of doing so. What are the chances of seeing one, anyway? Not good. I'm deep in the area, though, so if it happens it happens and I'll deal with my emotions later. Meanwhile, there are plenty of butterflies coloring my idle thoughts and I saw two road-killed coyotes back on the highway.

BAKER CITY

Light breeze making it nice for walking, despite the heat. I'm beneath the Oregon Trail Interpretive Center looking for the Trail itself. It's here, they say, but I'm not finding it. The air is turning hazy and I'm feeling feverish. Someone I talked to thought a grass burn or forest fire. The sun is brutal here between wind gusts, and it's a long way to the Willamette Valley, the Blue Mountains wafting on the horizon. My pasty natural sunscreen is on thick, as if I'm wearing whiteface. No one out here to witness, though, not even the rattler who shed this crinkly skin on its way elsewhere.

JOHN DAY

The dry clarity of the John Day as it cuts through canyon walls. I need some of that clarity myself. Familiarity does not ameliorate fact. I've been on this road a long time. . . . Found camp down the road from John Day, where I'm all set up by the water. Sometimes you have to stop to remember why you have to stop. . . . How bad can it be when you can sleep through the night knowing there are trees above you and a river within rock-throwing distance? Evergreens scattered randomly over the hillsides, it's greener here than I ever remember. No miles of sand and wobbly perceptions, but it's a lot more desert than the forests indicate when you wander into their midst. I am constantly reminded how little I know. The sense of scale here humbles.

STEENS MOUNTAIN

The mountain shoots up out of the ground without even looking quite like a mountain. Sheer faces of curving ridge—enveloping you rather than posing as something you look *at*—you don't focus on it as much as you allow it to permeate your attention, and in this it is an analogy for Oregon itself. Oregon's beauty, the diffuse heart that is all around you when you take a look: an antelope bounding parallel your car through the sagebrush, hiking the Little Blitzen in a gorge between rises, the aspen leaves glittering in the summer wind, the river rushing heavy by. Walking with the sun on your back and the grass at your knees in this ancient place.

PETROGLYPH LAKE

You can see all the way to nowhere in all directions from the road in. Petroglyph Lake appears right at the moment you give up on finding it. A quiet lake that announces nothing. The glyphs wait for you if you can find them, they've been waiting for some time.

HART MOUNTAIN

I imagine that people have died out here. The lakes below the mountain speak of nothing but more water . . . eventually . . . something green, that abundant valley promised—the dream of the Edenic West still a dream.

CRATER LAKE

The blue isn't bottomless, only 1,932 feet. But if you fell from the surface the time it would take to hit bottom might as well be forever. From the rim above, you feel yourself sinking in—it's the navel, where everything could fall in and keep falling.

MOUNT PISGAH

After the false summit, the true one: there's Jed's Sighting Pedestal, and there's the Kesey Farm right down there, where I'd like to lay my eyes on the bus Furthur. The mountain itself is a grassy afternoon, the land that butts up against private properties is dense Oregon forest, suitably enchanted. I proceed bushwhacking and what I get is scratched all up by blackberry bushes. A patch of moss-dripped wonder, the very picture of mysteries that end well, endings that stay mysteries. Tired, sweaty, bleeding, and satisfied, I return, adventure justifying its own cost.

SILVER FALLS

North Falls from a distance is an ideal falls cut out of a patterned wall of evergreens—a child's drawing of "a falls in a forest." Middle North Falls is the jewel, a walking path carved into the rock behind it allows you to see the world through the falls. It's the shift in perspective you might hope for from a "nature experience." Drake Falls, next, is a rapid-like gradual tumble of twenty-seven feet. This park as a whole speaks of fall for some reason (and not just as homonym)—maybe forests always speak of fall, dense green Oregon ones anyway, the cooling portending cooling, things coming to a close, still very much alive. It's crowded, a mixture of bother and good news. I return to what's around me.

TABLE ROCK

Going slow and attending to observation. After all, I'm out here. Drove out of Molalla on mostly unmarked roads, found a turnoff and drove up gravel for miles to nowhere, where I'm now hiking amidst many flies and one bull snake so far. Must stay moving (flies). I pick up a walking stick, which gives me confidence vs. hypothetical cougars. But after walking a ways up the fear evaporates. From the summit, no signs of humans except patches of clear cut on the surrounding hills. I keep thinking about the past, how sublime Oregon still is (in the Burkean sense) and what it looked like before we did things like clear cutting. Things that are gone. Things that aren't mine and never will be. Things my grandfather might have seen. But here now today I have views of Hood and Jefferson and they're all mine. I haven't seen another person all day. So remote once again so close to the city. I have miles to hike and miles to drive and it's all Oregon. I stop at a small river below Table Rock and put my feet in the cold water. Toes cramped in hiking shoes coming back to barefoot life. I want to stay in this as long as it will keep me.

WALDO LAKE

How distinctly Northwest this lake, in the thick-forest, bumpy-terrain sense of the word. Not spectacular but confident and stable. The water laps reassuringly below the bench where I sit, sun getting ready to set directly across the water from me. It's pleasantly cool here and will probably be fully chilly tonight. I don't know why I picked this lake for tonight, except that it reminds me of Emerson and it's sometimes nice to be reminded of Emerson. So here I am at lakeshore all alone eating a banana, listening to the water. Life no longer all in front of me but all around me, and from any number of perspectives that is what a person could go looking for and be satisfied to find, content to sit and gaze and remember and reflect and be patient forever patient.

DEVILS LAKE

The inner narrator goes silent in the face of sudden beauty.

Impressions register but they don't survive the leap into language. One passing cyclist (and there are many passing cyclists) describes the water as "crazy green." Aqua mixes viscously with turquoise and even old blue, all of it glistening delicately as a light wind jostles the surface. We go slowly as we go gratefully onward.

LAVA LAKE

I continue down the road to Lava and Little Lava Lakes, where after the day's first hike I'm putting my dirty feet in the clean water. Despite a yeoman's effort with the sunscreen and regular use of hats I've developed a slight burn—probably due to the altitude. This area's been logged heavily. I've seen trucks full of timber—and I've noted how many trees it takes these days to fill up a load and wondered where they came from. It could have been here. Total clear cut saved only by the trees that were too small to take. It's more foresty this way—but barely. What to say? We use places up. Sitting by Little Lava Lake I discover the ants to be black, meaty, and in healthy supply. Standing a moment later in the same lake, several small fish and one good-sized trout swim over to investigate me. I'm back to flip-flops, and while my feet thank me, they do get dusty. Several scrape marks on trees, too, where bucks rub their antlers. The wake of our destruction doesn't make me angry today as much as lonely. I could get on a plane and leave this all behind. But I'm here to continue. Reason for hope, to get and to give.

HJ ANDREWS EXPERIMENTAL FOREST

At dusk, I look up to see a rabbit hop by and compose a little note to a friend: *I'm watching rabbits outside my window. / They are not distractions / from the work to be done; / they are its impetus.* Darkness comes suddenly and completely. Sitting here reading about cougars I find myself looking for two yellow eyes in the black. This blood is western blood and there is so much to be grateful for.

BLUE RIVER

A steep climb down the embankment and then this small river carved out of time itself. Worn holes distinguish an otherwise subtle Northwest river, sinking many feet, their banks rising to water's surface—everything fully transparent. I walk across the river jumping over the holes and onto the rocks, some of which rise above the surface and some of which are inches below. Some of the lingering dust and mud has thereby been cleared from my boots. Two deer, earlier, saw me turn a corner and bounded gracefully down a mountainside that would take a person an hour to traverse (forget grace). Did see a nice thick garter snake near the creek, too. Deep in the woods, sitting alone, everything as I'd choose it, the creek rushing down from the ridge, there's a part of me that's still not at ease. It's a small part, a quiet voice, but it is there and it keeps talking. The trick, I assume, is not to silence it but to leave it alone.

CLEAR LAKE

Set up the tent and had just enough time to walk by the water and see part of a pink and peach sky fade. In the morning I'll get up and walk around the lake, paying special attention to the head of the McKenzie. There's something about this area that strikes a deep chord in me. I'm calibrated to Oregon, this Oregon especially, and when I'm somewhere else for too long I feel out of alignment. Is that too much? It's just that there is part of me—an important part—that's happy here. There is no wind, no clouds, it's not dark enough for stars yet. It's warm still and the bugs aren't biting. The camp host is next to me running some kind of generator. Besides that, no sounds but for occasional birds.

Up at first light to hike the lake, it must be early, as no one else in the camp is up yet. Half-way through the night I got into rather than on top of my sleeping bag. By morning it was almost chilly outside the tent, with moisture that came from I can't tell where. Here I am now at the head of the McKenzie, light rapids white-noising just so far down. I'm content to sit here awhile.

SAHALIE FALLS

The falls sounds in the parking lot and the mist reaches almost as far. The water drops from the ledge faster than mere gravity can account for. Sheets of water in hallucinogenic patterns. The rainbow above the pool so strong and so natural as to seem permanent. A magical spot on the water's journey from the McKenzie to the Willamette, Columbia, Pacific, clouds, rain, home.

OPAL CREEK

Oregon summer. What does the human being
need that is not provided?

METOLIUS SPRINGS

That spirit of the Northwest, that richness—the profusion of *life,* sex mixed up in it—so much production you want to participate, spill out, overflow create create create to be like this river emerging from the earth full flowing. It isn't there, then it is. You haven't seen a blue jay until you've seen a blue jay. Joyous thump of my heart when I look into these pinewoods, when the quietness is the type that promises to bust with . . . my mood is the sound the river makes. It's mythology as wellspring—beauty, natural beauty, but us necessary to make it through observation "beautiful." Does the tree make a sound? The river does. I hear it. I am here in nature is here in me, we are in this together this is in us—the water flows upward now—why not?—the mountain, Jefferson, downstream, up there across the field all of my vision reaches and reaches and grabs hold (the blue jay!) the meadow the dry sunshine on my dust-caked toes—on the road, wheels pointed at the present it goes and it goes, wheels turning me into whatever I can think of and I can think of everything out here where the evergreens point ever up and stillness speaks above a crystal water spring.

PAINTED HILLS

Caroll Rim. "Proceed no further," reads the sign at the half-mile trail's end. These hills are still sacred—one of the few places that are—the ribbons of color wrapped around sloping mounds of untouched land, the history right on the surface to see. Red and green minerals. Blue at midday harder to locate. The air is *dry* and the sun feels good, powerful, and character building. Time is roughly still when the wind pauses briefly. There's a largeness here, an isolated one. I see no one else for miles on these hills. The ground effects a three-dimensional topographic map, the lines force an understanding of elevation and history. Rattlesnakes have been here five million years; native peoples, ten thousand; us . . . the wind is trying to get me to leave.

Painted Cove. Bump of a hill. Green and red

sections. Close enough to make out texture. It's dry and crumbly, though it looks like soft moss from even a short distance. A kind of clay. A red-beaked hawk circling above the car. Why does no one vandalize a place like this? What prevents them? A couple of pines make nice shade. The quietness here is a kind of mental space.

TRILLIUM LAKE

Fat wet flakes, skis sticking to the ground. So quiet here. The impression is you can hear forever, but the snow muffles even nearby sounds. Vibrations loosen piled snow from branches; it lands in great poofs fanning out as if the spray of a crashed wave. Looking up into the sky there is no sense of perspective, distance, time—there is nothing to contrast anything with until a flake touches your skin, startling, focusing, clarifying. The visual field is overwhelmed. Color has no meaning. The lake is heavy with accumulated snow. There's a dock across. It beckons with idyllic promises of dogs and sweaters and cocoa. I fall a few times magnificently. I don't want to be lyrical about it. I'd rather just ski in the snow and not have to think about too much. A crow flaps audibly over my head.

SKIBOWL

It's a great good feeling to be out riding fresh powder. The rhythm of the movement comes quickly back. The roll of the slope, the sink of the snow, the distance of the cold. Snow snows until it doesn't, then it's gray on bright when the clouds break and there's the summit, Hood glowing just about radiant above. My goodness. Up on the ridgeline the snow is heavy, deep with powder. I fall slowly until I am submerged. I feel entombed, restricted—but also held. Above me the fog is thick, trees protrude like dark lines on a white map, a kind of communication.

LOST LAKE BUTTE

Mount Hood, iconic Oregon mountain, never bigger in my field of vision. Either I've been on it and too close to see it or I've been so far away that it shrinks in the distance to only sometimes float above Portland. It's big now and looks more like a mountain than any mountain ever has, not floating but jutting right out of the ground. It's connected at all points substantially, as if the foothills said to themselves, "Enough screwing around, let's really do something here." The snow-capped peak, the slow-moving glaciers, the timberline and forests below, the canyon-making rivers, the land rising again and rolling on up to the ground beneath my feet. How lucky we are.

LOST LAKE

Sitting by the campfire a little before dark. Just the right kind of air. Drinking a Zigzag River Lager, which seems appropriate. Emily Dickinson says, "Nature is what we know— / Yet have no art to say—" The questions that confound humankind once do so indefinitely: Why are we here at all? Why are we *we*? The beauty is in the question and the courage is in maintaining without answers, and so we have art and so we turn to nature, two places where the lack of answer is articulated back to us, voicing the reality we access as the particular species of mammalian carbon-based lifeforms each of us is. From where I'm sitting it looks like this: the fire's almost out but there's more wood I can add when I'm ready, the trees are swaying above me like pleasantly drunk friends standing up too fast, in the distance there are voices—I

can't make out what they're saying but they are
talk talk talk—there is so much still to say.

ONEONTA

A few people at the trailhead on the Old Columbia Highway, no one else in the water as I wade through the creek up Oneonta Gorge. Alone. Quite a thing to know a place like this. The water is cool but not distressingly so, and only reaches waist deep in a couple of pools. A living wall on the gorge's face where water drips and mists like a gentle shower over moss-covered rocks. Life here fills every void. The place is lush, the mist off the falls teases my neck and head. My guard is open to the elements and these forces. Water wears away rock, moss grows soft, trees umbrella out over the sky opening above. If my feet were ever cold they aren't now. There are secrets that stay secrets because you can't share them even if you try, which is fine.

JAPANESE GARDEN

I can see the mountain from here, suspended. Portland lies between—its tallest buildings not reaching even the base of Hood from this perspective. This is a quiet time of year and though I'm thinking about various things, my mind is muted and my thinking is leisurely, no more rushed than a falling leaf. No more directed either. The leaf—a maple—lands on the water's surface, where it will sink and rot. Beautiful words are a problem only if they are not true. We need true words, true like the snake-curve of a worn path or the flow of water over rocks. It's okay to be cold sometimes and drink warm drinks after, as I will soon. The thoughts I'm thinking are like many before them and many to follow them. The moss on the ground is soft. My cell phone has been turned off for hours. I remember why I was angry earlier, but I am no longer angry. There is a hut to my right. I used to skip school when it was raining and sit in that hut. I remember those days fondly. This is a life. The soothing patter of rain on wood. Mushrooms sprouting between stones in the walk. A woman takes my picture. The thing is not to represent, the thing is to touch with spirit. To communicate is to set two souls vibrating at the same frequency. There is magic all around us. I submit.

FOREST PARK

I literally cannot contain my exuberance this day, but who needs containment? It erupts. These profound woods, this mild heat, this joyful body ecstasis.

COUNCIL CREST

One of the plaques here reads, in part:

The rivers today, still central to transportation and trade, also bring nature to the heart of the city. Salmon runs and nesting herons lift the spirit of the people who live here. The river reminds us of vital connections—the natural to the man-made, the timeless to the new.

It's a quiet afternoon, nearly summer. There doesn't always have to be so much to say.

I'm going to walk some more in these woods.

NOSTALGIAS

What do you mean you can't *remake* the past?

Of course you can.

The Last Westerners, meaning us, standing in Astoria, nowhere to go but back, not even an escape but a retreat. And so if I must retreat let me *re*treat . . .

Our narratives are always looking back. John Locke . . . Thomas Jefferson . . . Lewis and Clark . . . culminating in the speaker here at the mouth of the Columbia facing an unconquerable sea confident in the enumerated rights in my back pocket. The course of empire steadily takes its westward way . . . the story ending where the speaker's feet meet the ground. These Oregon

Trails could have led elsewhere, but then they wouldn't be "Oregon" trails, and destiny might have manifested a thousand like contingencies. An argument, a claim, an adventure succeeds because it succeeded, and only. A story lingers in memory as circumstances allow and only insofar as it bears on the present. The same is true for the future that we call upon in order to live out the day: "God has a plan"; "It'll work out in the end"; "In 10,000 years we'll all be dead and these struggles won't amount to nothing." We see even the future in hindsight: from *after God's plan is enacted, after it has worked out, after we have been wiped from the planet.*

But life takes place before the stories are written, and I take little reassurance from the fact that the events I'm describing will eventually be reducible to narrative. It's always the time before some story, some other story, has started. And yet when danger palpitates in us, when we encounter the sublime, when we are startled to wake in a flooded tent—to put in general terms: when we gather experiences—we wonder which story (or maybe which essay) we are living in.

Having no story in which to arrange one's experiences? There is no worse fortune.

There is a light snow falling outside my Minnesota window. Two crows on the icy ground, centered in the walnut frame, make a picture of the north country as unwelcoming landscape. The elements encroach on the empty gray parking lot and time hangs brittle on the air. Dreams stretch languidly indoors, the dreaming itself (not the dreamed) the real pleasure. I luxuriate here.

See, I'm thinking about home and what

it means and how to get there. So indulge me a moment while I go on staring out the window—the cat alongside me doing the same, patient and unimpressed by our gray horizons—and think of home.

It is a kind of nostalgia that comprises a montage of personal history, a random or not so random assortment of moments: a scene from Little League in which I was the hero; one time when I caught my little sister looking up to me with pride; those days in high school when everything was happening all at once and there was no way to contain the moment inside one merely human body; the night in Eugene's Alton-Baker Park when I first took hallucinogenic drugs and felt-watched time go all gooey on me—all of it adding up to, the question is what.

The way you must leave home to find it is the way you find your voice only in silence—indeed require silence to have a voice. The cat turns from staring out the window at crows to watch me stare out the window at crows. The temperature is low, snow no longer falling, ice building on the cement ground. Nothing really moves. The crows are gone.

Something's gonna happen and something has happened and something will go on happening and where've you been and what'll you do.

If my generation is the first generation (in a while) that won't move up a little from our parents', maybe we won't remain as nostalgic either. It's possible that we'll come to see in our youth not mere innocence but negligence as well. We, who were raised on fast food and cheap oil, might decide to no longer accept that no one knew about future costs, that the matter wasn't ignorance but indifference. I see it both ways. Some days I want to teach the past a lesson about consequences while trying to improve the future. And some days I want to eat at McDonald's and hasten the apocalypse.

Nothing speaks more directly to me of the assurances of the past than McDonald's. I haven't eaten one of their burgers in years; nevertheless, when I see one (or, more powerfully, when I smell one) I am taken immediately back to my childhood. I am in my aunt's station wagon—I, who have known only hamburgers and cheeseburgers—fascinated as my cousin orders Chicken McNuggets and dips them in, of all things, honey . . . the summer they offer basketball cards if you order a big enough bucket of soda pop and I eat lunch there every day until I have the full set . . . the last time I eat there before giving up meat. Thinking about it now, I can taste, can *feel*, one of their cheeseburgers in my mouth.

Any disparaging remark you would make about McDonald's I would make too. And yet, I will always love, and I do mean *love*, McDonald's.

Before nostalgia was a wistful longing for the past it was a severe homesickness. Severe, even crippling. But what happens when *a wistful longing for the past* isn't a condition some people have any more than air is just something some people breathe?

The term *nostalgia* was coined by Johannas Hofer, a Swiss doctor, in 1688. Early treatments for nostalgia included leeches, warm hypnotic emulsions, opium. I have tried only one of these remedies, which I found, in its short-term obliteration of symptoms, effective.

However, nostalgia strikes not only persons but peoples—the *demos*, and in its democracy it reveals a society uprooted. What are we but a people on the move away from, on our way to, but whatever else ever restless?

When first diagnosed, nostalgia affected soldiers who missed their homelands. The United States of America did not experience an outbreak until our Civil War. In the twentieth century, it became a condition of longing for one's childhood. If Freud is right that to return home is to analyze one's early traumas, then to long to return is to know oneself as a suffering being.

Later, nostalgia became a lack of manliness, a form of weakness finding easy resonance with the

Puritan fear of idleness. It is true, you can be too busy for nostalgia, but no essayist, whose trade is plied of leisure, has ever known this condition.

Enamored of distance . . . luxuriating in long-ing . . . disinclined toward completion . . . "the nostalgic directs his gaze not only backward but sideways, and expresses himself in elegiac poems and ironic fragments, not in philosophical or scientific treatises. Nostalgia remains unsystem-atic and unsynthesizable; it seduces rather than convinces."

So Svetlana Boym gives us one way of think-ing about how things might have been as these provisional claims accumulate . . .

. . . the conditions are the conditions . . . my world is credit cards and plastic and social media and air conditioning . . . and I may criticize these things in moral terms (in fact, I do), but they are my things . . . maybe we've already wrecked our environment . . . and yet: Where do we find ourselves? Where will we go?

The nostalgist is on shaky ground, of course, when he mentions morality, he who will gladly give up the past that doesn't suit his ends.

One may escape, though, or disappear: online, where place is meaningless (as long as the wifi's working), and time is too. Entertainment as opiate, distraction as divinity. ADHD as epidemic, epidemic as adaptation, adaptation as proof that what doesn't kill us . . .

But the faster the world becomes one thing, the more nostalgia we have for when it was many. All things considered, the nostalgic would rather not be flattened by the universal (be it God, Progress, or the Internet).

It's not that life (technology and all the rest)

is changing too fast for us keep up, it's that the concept of holding on to anything has become so foreign. The faster we experience change the less the changes seem to mean anything at all. And yet, as things are inevitably replaced other things are irrevocably lost.

The nostalgic, then, is he for whom the past is of value to the present as past.

According to Novalis, "Philosophy is really a homesickness; it is an urge to be at home everywhere." I have no desire to be at home everywhere. I want only to be at home *at home*. But home is so far away from wherever I am I can only be at home in my awayness, in this perpetual longing.

This paradox is at the core of distance, of time,

of difference, of self. But paradoxes are mental symptoms of which the body is free. Soon, when I'm done here, I'll go out and go for a walk. A few blocks from my window is a lake I've circled hundreds of times over the past few years. I think I'll circle it again, listen to the snow crunch under my boots, and see if I can find myself on the ground again, somewhere on the shoreline, a part of *this* world.

One of the dangers of nostalgia is it can idealize and reify a nonexistent reality—it thereby risks becoming religion or ideology. But as Americans, pragmatism in our blood, we know that our commitments are always provisional—even our commitments to the past. We will give them up the moment circumstances require us to.

The nostalgia that focuses on the longing itself more than the impossible home doubts the absolute Truth that home promises. The attentive individual has heard such promises before and taken note. He lives now as he reflects: suspended in doubt, learning to smile.

There's nothing to return to and yet we want to return—our nostalgia exists unto itself. We long *despite* having no object of longing (*despite* being a politer way here of saying *because*).

Nostalgia wants to erase the borders between now and then, between here and there, wants to erase all borders; ultimately, it desires the peace of non-existence—or the next best substitute: cessation.

Except: I long, therefore I am.

Nostalgia is always self-perpetuating because its real function is not to return to a past that is gone (and indeed never was) but to feel pleasure in the longing itself. In its self-perpetuation it pretends—like all addictions—to want to be self-defeating. Just get me back there, it says, and

I will be happy—but the greatest lie of nostalgia has always been that there was a time before nostalgia.

Where do we find ourselves, we must constantly ask after Emerson. Where do we find ourselves? Without looking back, we don't. As the eye does not see the eye and the blade does not slice the blade, there is no identity without difference, no individual without environment, no time outside time.

No time outside time. The past we yearn for contains within it a prior past, and so on to time immemorial. The vague or not so vague longing is not for lost happiness (though we may comfort ourselves imagining so), it is for the assurance we project through hindsight: those events, those experiences have become *this story*.

The search for lost time, the search for lost places is the desire to be lost in a story that has a happy enough ending (and every backward glance is from the end of *a* tunnel). We don't look back when the menace is at our heels. When the cougar is at my throat, I fight; it's only after I've survived (if I've survived) that I look back.

When Sandy and I decided to move for a while to the Midwest prairie, my mother, eastern Montana still in her bones after half a lifetime in Portland, wove each of us a scarf and said good luck. My scarf has served me well on days the air's been cold enough to burn exposed skin. It's draped over my chair now, ready to be wrapped around my neck when I go out and in all likelihood dream of mountains and oceans and forests and deserts, dream of walking on soggy ground and running my hands over familiar textures: the dew on jagged fern leaves, the chunky bark of a Doug-fir. I see myself as a boy standing in the wind and sideways mist at Ecola State Park watching the whales go by, wandering into the woods to uncover salamanders—salamanders I so rarely see now.

We know now that it is possible, even common, to feel homesick and sick of home at once. What we long for is not a home but a reunion with ourselves that doesn't occur in a place, not to mention not at all.

The past isn't what happened but how I remember it; the future isn't what will happen but how the past will later look.

There is no nothing here but what it means to be a human being—a human being looking forward and back—every looking forward a looking back and every looking back a looking forward—that's what home means and you can never go back there, never be there, can never even have been there—we are human and what we stand to regain is a search itself—not a tautology then but a tangled process of becoming.

Writing doesn't have to mean a search for lost home (call it time or place or innocence), but so often it does. Marina Tsvetaeva says all poets are Jews. Aren't we all exiles trying to return to a home that no longer exists, if it ever did?

My Portland is the city as I know it: Grant Park, Irvington, Laurelhurst, Hollywood; the logical grid of the Northeast Portland streets; the parks—Wilshire, Fernhill, Rose City—where I would ride my bike as a kid and that I run to now. My history, my associations, my memories: the Trail Blazers of the Rip City era; my fourth-grade class field trip to the opening of the Convention Center. I remember when the first MAX line went in; I remember when North and inner Northeast had black neighborhoods where it just so happened we had no reason to visit; I remember when Powell's was still surrounded by warehouses. More memories: the Japanese Garden, Forest Park—places I used to hang out when I was skipping school by myself; bagel shops, coffee shops—places I used to hang out when I was skipping school with friends; Nature's, before it was Wild Oats, before it was Whole Foods, before it was Amazon, where I used to work as a bagger—after my shifts summer nights I'd drink microbrews with artists and hippies and socialists and vegans who I was lucky to learn from. I could go on. Shall I go on? My mom used to take my sister and me to visit a friend in Northwest who lived across the street from the best play structure in town (Couch Park); she took us also to Lower Macleay Park, where we followed Balch Creek and climbed up under the Thurman Street Bridge to play; we fed the ducks at Laurelhurst Park. All

the places we partied in high school: Arbo, Ensbo, Witch's, Ditler's, Swan Island, and so on, half the fun being the escape when the cops arrived. More: Elliott Smith shows at LaLuna, Proz and Conz at the Roseland; sneaking into Lloyd Center during cross-country workouts knowing security could never catch us; working at the mall—Woody serving tacos, Jamie scooping ice cream, Garon and James renting out ice skates, Bill selling movie tickets, and me unpacking boxes at the GAP; hiking with girlfriends in the Columbia River Gorge; the early fumblings with sex; the expectations, the negotiations, and the realities. I could go on and on. It adds up to the usual thing—the beginning of a life—experienced in the usual manner: taken for granted, left behind, and eventually longed for.

My Portland is at times as distant cities were to Montaigne: "the Rome and Paris that I have in my soul . . . without size and without place, without stone, without plaster, and without wood." It lives as an idea. Ideas. Memories. Yet when I arrive there I am struck by particularity. I pluck and chew peppermint and spearmint leaves from my parents' garden and the wild things they do in my mouth leave me dissatisfied with language and thoughts.

As long as a myth is useful, it's a good myth.

But the West fails as a myth. So self-satisfied, it cannot accommodate the discovery that the certainties of youth are not so certain. Eventually the justifications run out and we must, each of us, get through the night anew.

I hear the drum of steady rain when I close my eyes. Oregon is neither a paradise I can arrive at nor a home I can return to.

In America, where we believe in nothing so much as the future we will this time make perfect, nostalgia becomes the yin to our optimism's yang. Confronted by the waste of our past futures, we yearn for a time when our myth of pure possibility lay more purely in the unblemished ahead.

We aren't supposed to be so past-conscious, we forward-lookers, we progress-believers. Our ancestors (or we ourselves) went west for a reason. For opportunity. For freedom. For prosperity. But after we've been here a while and we have or do not have (it doesn't really matter) these things, we see that what we long for is the possibility of having them. We want the promise more than the actual. The American Dream is of conquering, not of having conquered but of conquering (the native peoples, the land, limitations of all kinds).

We don't want to have won; we want to be winning. We want, that is, for the game never to end. But since the game is ending as it is always ending we take refuge in the memory of an earlier time when there was even more progress to make.

But weightlessness is its own burden, and we self-definers, self-creators know the strain. Nostalgia is the unrelenting feeling that mad-dash progress comes at a cost. We idealize the past all the more as we rush faster by the minute away from it. Being American means in this respect that life will always be a bit like Christmas: a letdown from unreasonable expectations, but always somehow also better in retrospect.

The other side of perpetual progress is a mourning of times we failed to appreciate when we had the chance because we were in such a mad rush to get *here,* which upon disinterested consideration doesn't appear to be all it was cracked up to be. And we haven't yet learned how to sit still. I'm at my desk here and I'm trying for once to be very still.

JUST STAY

At the end of every trip home to Oregon there comes a moment just before it's time for Sandy and me to join the security check line at PDX when we make eye contact and each of us is weakened by the nostalgic pull of this place. Here is where we first met and flirted and, by great luck, eventually married. Here is where our friends and family ask with respectful optimism if we'll return for good, where we say we will get back to when circumstances allow it. Here is where our *I*s as well as our *we* were largely forged. And since we are more or less happy, it's natural to idealize the cradle of our past. No other *here* could ever compete.

As we near the metal detector, one of us says, "What if we don't get on the plane? What if we just stay?" This is a cruel thing to say, but inevitably we say it. As a matter of course, this urge to remain, which is really an urge to return, falls in the afterglow of a week or more comprising trips to the Cascades and the Pacific, nights spent under family roof again, visits to Powell's, hikes through Forest Park, kayak paddles down the Tualatin, and on and on, coffee with friends as soft rain touches window.

It's not fair to judge the future by this past, that place by this, but still we remind ourselves of everything we're leaving, as if to ensure a confrontation with the fear that the longer we're away the less likely we'll one day get back. Of course, we realize there is no coming back, there is no *here* even to come back to. The accretion of new relationships and experiences *there* are slowly overwhelming *here* and the longing, the visceral longing, for Oregon. What's lost to us, then, is not Oregon but certain versions of ourselves

Acknowledgments

First, thanks to Victoria Blanco, Bridget Mendel, and Florencia Lauria, who have been by my side with these essays from the beginning.

My profound appreciation to David Oates, whose wise editorial judgement and direction were instrumental in helping this book take its final form, and whose confidence in the project enabled it to find its way into the world. Alex Hirsch read this book in manuscript and knew exactly the art that should accompany it. Steve Connell had the vision for how it could all come together into this handsomely designed book. Thank you, Alex and Steve.

Thanks also to Patricia Hampl, Madelon Sprengnether, Julie Schumacher, Dan Philippon, perpetually overcome. And if we're nostalgic, if I'm nostalgic by disposition, it's because here is never as *here* as I dream. The security line leads us forward, and when the plane departs—as it always departs—we're on it.

ABOUT THE AUTHOR

Scott F. Parker is the author of *Running After Prefontaine: A Memoir* and the editor of *Conversations with Joan Didion* and *Conversations with Ken Kesey*, among other books. His writing has appeared in *Tin House, Philosophy Now, The Believer Logger, Portland Monthly*, and other publications. Parker is the copyeditor for Hawthorne Books and teaches writing at Montana State University. Born and raised in Oregon, he lives in Bozeman with his wife, their son, and Mavis the cat. Find him online at scottfparker.com.

ABOUT THE ARTIST

Raised in Chicago, Alex Hirsch received a Bachelor of Arts with Honors and Bachelor of Fine Arts Magna Cum Laude from the University of Michigan, and a Master of Fine Arts from Washington University. She makes her home in the Pacific Northwest where she specializes in making painterly architectural art glass and watercolors on paper. Her work is in national and international collections including the United States Embassy (Bulgaria), Good Samaritan Hospital, Oregon State University, U.S. Aid (Uganda), Hallmark Corporation, ODS Companies, and Southern Oregon University. Find her online at AlexHirschArt.com.

J. Fossenbell, and everyone else at the University of Minnesota who offered valuable feedback on these essays.

Mary and Ralph Bramucci taught me that the heart of Oregon was out there for me to discover. I thank Mary and remember Ralph for the models they've been for me.

My greatest thanks to Sandy, *sine qua non*.

Thanks also to the following publications, where versions of these essays first appeared: *Oregon Quarterly* online ("On the Gentle Sand Facing In"); *Sport Literate:* "Free and Easy Wandering on the Pacific Crest Trail"; *Oregon Humanities:* "Just Stay"; *Wander Lost Review* ("Going Home").